TOULOUSE

Text written in association with
Claudine Roland
Translated by
Ann MacDonald-Plénacoste

◀ *The Chaussée du Bazacle (Bazacle Ford) and the chapel dome of La Grave Hospital. "Bazacle" comes from the Latin word for a ford.*

▲▲ *The statue of the Roman Emperor Marc Aurèle found at Martres-Tolosane, Musée Saint-Raymond.*

▲ *The Cross of Toulouse, keystone of the "Raymond VI" nave, Cathedral of Saint Étienne.*

▶ *A Romanesque marble low-relief, Saint Sernin Basilica.*

THE GOLDEN AGE OF TOULOUSE

A river flowing into the Atlantic, easy access to the Mediterranean Sea, a pleasant climate, fertile land…, the advantages of this bank of the Garonne river have attracted Man since the Neolithic Age. Toulouse was founded in the 3rd century B.C. by the Volques Tectosages who came from the forests of Bohemia. But in spite of their refined civilization, they had to give way to the Romans in the year 118 B.C. *Tolosa* became a prosperous Roman colony: in the 2nd century A.D., it was the second largest town in the Narbonne region of Gaul with over 20 000 inhabitants and a surface-area of 90 hectares. Christianism developed there but the invasions by Barbarian tribes marked the beginning of hard times… In 418, the Visigoths made Toulouse the capital of a vast kingdom stretching from the Loire to Gibraltar. Alaric II, their king, was defeated by Clovis at the battle of Vouillé in 507. Under the Merovingians and then the Carolingians, Toulouse was part of Aquitaine and time passed uneventfully until the 11th century when the town took on a new lease of life. At this time, the Counts of Toulouse were extending their domination to the South. In 1096, Raymond IV even led one of the armies of the first crusade. The Pope gave his benediction on this occasion and consecrated the new church of Saint Sernin at the same time. The *bourgeoisie* gradually acquired more

3

power and these future *capitouls* (municipal magistrates) formed a "Common Council" to manage municipal affairs. Catharism spread quickly in this prosperous society and the cursaders who hurtled South to fight the heresay were also attracted by the town's wealth… besieged and then occupied, Toulouse took sides with Raymond VI; Simon de Montfort, leader of the Crusaders, was killed in 1218. But the autonomy of the Counts was drawing to a close… In 1271, Toulouse, bastion of the Catholic faith, became part of the royal domain. During the 15th and 16th centuries, the town grew rich due to the trading of *pastel*, a plant used to produce a blue dye which was in great demand. Its leaves, rolled into husks, brought great wealth to the region… until the arrival of American indigo. Economic difficulties and religious wars weakened the city during the centuries which followed and Toulouse did not recover until the 18th century. Relying on the land and trading in corn, it was relatively untouched by the industrial revolution… In 1917, the Latécoère factory – which later became the Airmail Postal Service – was set up far from the battle front. The prestigious Toulouse aeronautical industry was born. Today, Toulouse has over one hundred thousand inhabitants and is the second largest French university town. Resolutely facing the future, it nevertheless retains the memory of its rich past…

◀ *Attic windows of the mill of the Château Narbonnais, jardin des Plantes (Botanical Gardens). The Château Narbonnais, residence of the Counts of Toulouse, was situated on the site of the present law-courts and was demolished in the 16th century.*

▶ *Portrait of a "capitoul" by Guillaume Cammas, Musée du Vieux-Toulouse. The artist, an official of the town, was also an architect and designed the frontage of the Capitole.*

▲ *The "Ville Rose" is also the city of violets. They are to be found in bouquets, sweets, perfume… As early as the 14th century, literary competitions, forerunners of the famous "Jeux Floraux", were organised in the tradition of the troubadours and the winning poet was always awarded a golden violet.*

◀ *Husk drier, Château-musée de Magrin (Tarn). The "pastel", grown in the Albigeois and Lauragais regions, brought fortune to the Toulouse traders.*

◀ *The Tour de Serta (Serta Tower), rue Saint-Rome. This twenty-three metre high tower crowning a half-timbered house, was built by the "capitoul" Pierre de Serta as a mark of his social success…*

▶ *The new Airbus models spread their wings on the Toulouse skyline. From Clément Ader to the giant of the European aeronautics industry: a century of passion.*

5

▲ *The right bank of the Garonne and the Pont-Neuf. A symphony of pink and blue...*

◀ *The low-relief of the Ponts-Jumeaux (Twin Bridges). In the 18th century, the architect Saget decided to use a single structure to span the two canals (the Midi and the Brienne). The sculptor François Lucas decorated these twin bridges with a low-relief symbolizing the union of the Atlantic and the Mediterranean.*

▶ *The Canal de Brienne. An invitation for a stroll...*

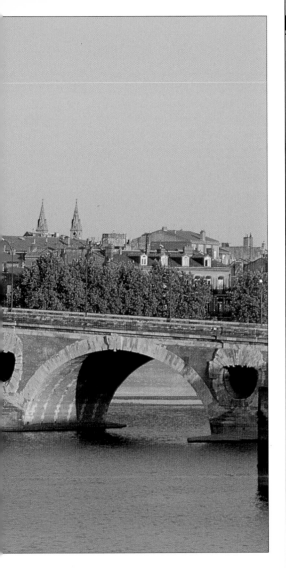

A RIVER AND CANALS

I t is difficult to imagine that this capricious river was once a busy navigation route! Toulouse is tenderly encircled by an arm of the Garonne; However, although the town was indeed born because of its river, the two have not always lived in perfect harmony. A source of wealth because it had enabled profitable trading since ancient times, the river also brought its share of misfortune: invasions and especially flooding. The famous Pont-Neuf (the New Bridge) was the first to resist the river's anger. It was begun in 1544 and inaugurated in... 1659 by Louis XIV. One century and four architects were necessary to complete this colossal structure. The two towers of the triumphal arch which used to decorate it were removed during the 19th century because they hindered traffic... In order to increase corn trading, Pierre Paul de Riquet, a hydraulics specialist, designed and built a canal, two hundred and forty-one kilometres long, finally linking Toulouse to the Mediterranean. The Canal du Midi took scarcely fourteen years to build, from 1667 to 1681. One century later, the small Canal de Brienne (from the name of its promoter, Cardinal Loménie de Brienne) was constructed to link the Canal du Midi to the Garonne. But boats could not sail safely as far as Bordeaux until the Garonne lateral canal was opened in the 19th century.

7

▲▲ *Detail of the chevet of Saint-Sernin. The gentle polychromy of stone and brick is complemented by the warm colour of the roof tiles on the chapels.*

▲ *Saint-Sernin, sculpted capital of the Porte des Comtes (the Counts' gate), 11th century. The Porte des Comtes takes its name from the nearby funeral alcove housing the sarcophagi of the Counts of Toulouse.*

▶ *Saint-Sernin, tympanum of the Miègeville gate representing the Ascension of Christ.*

SAINT-SERNIN, THE IMPETUS OF FAITH

The largest Romanesque edifice (one hundred and fifteen metres long) and one of the most beautiful… Even today, Saint-Sernin is a surprise to visitors who wonder at the subtle marriage of brick and stone and at the astonishing association of the superposed rounded forms of its chevet, the source of its towering five-tiered bell-tower. Its story began around 250 A.D. The first Bishop of Toulouse, who was to become Saint Saturnin (or Saint Sernin) died as a martyr and was dragged by a bull for having refused to bow down to the pagan idols of the temple of the Capitole. According to legend, his body was buried by two Christians, the *Saintes Puelles.* At the beginning of the 5th century, his remains were taken to a church built on the site of the present basilica. The cult of Saint Saturnin developed and, towards the year one thousand, the church became an important point on the road to Saint-Jacques-de-Compostelle. In the 1060's, the canons decided to build a new church big enough to accommodate the flow of pilgrims…

In 1096, Pope Urban II, who had come to give his blessing to the departure of Count Raymond IV on the first crusade, consecrated the altar. Building work progressed rapidly at first under the responsibility of Raymond Gayrard, slowed down when he died in 1118 and was continued by Abbot Bernard de Gensac in the 13th century.

▲ *View of the Saint Sernin Basilica from the north-west. The massive west facade with its double gate and great rose-window is probably unfinished. The five recessed storeys and the association of brick and stone accentuate the elegance of the octagonal spire rising to a height of sixty-five metres.*

▶ *Saint-Sernin, statue of the apostle James, on the left of the tympanum of the Miègeville gate.*

A magnificent cloister and the outbuildings of the Abbey were demolished in the 19th century. The Renaissance outer gate is the last remaining vestige of the surrounding wall. With its long, narrow nave, wide aisles, vast transept and spacious ambulatory with numerous chapels, the basilica – a title given in 1878 – was easily able to accommodate the crowds of pilgrims. These pilgrims were not content to pray only to Saint Sernin (whose body now lies in a baroque sarcophagus above the altar); they carried out *a tour of saintly remains.* Indeed, several relics of other saints had been given to the Abbey for safe keeping. They can still be seen in the chapels, lying in richly sculpted 17th century cupboards. Two crypts also contain reliquaries and liturgical objects, a sumptuous treasure including, above all, the reliquary of the True Cross. During the 19th century, seven admirable low-reliefs representing Christ surrounded by a cherubin and a seraphin (probably the work of Bernard Gilduin, the craftsman who sculpted the marble altar dedicated to Urban II), angels and apostles were set into the wall surrounding the apse. Romanesque frescoes have recently been brought to light in the transept. Restored a little too personally by Viollet-le-Duc last century, Saint-Sernin has recently recovered the purity of its Romanesque architecture.

◀ *Saint-Sernin, inside the nave. The narrow central nave (eight metres sixty wide) intensifies the impression of height.*

▶ *Saint-Sernin, detail of one of the wooden stalls sculpted in the 17th century. Their luxuriant decoration was inspired by the furniture in the Cathedral of Saint Étienne.*

▶▶ *Saint-Sernin, the keystone of the upper crypt.*

◀ *Saint-Sernin, reliquary treasure of the True Cross. This superb reliquary in enamelled copper was made in Limoges at the end of the 12th century. The front represents Jerusalem and John, Abbot of Notre-Dame de Josaphat, giving the relic to Raimond Botardel, a Toulouse lawyer. The top depicts the Saintly Women at the Tomb.*

◀◀ *Saint-Sernin, detail of a 12th century Romanesque fresco illustrating the resurrection of Christ. Christ is enthroned at the top of the illustration.*

▶ *Saint-Sernin, Christ enthroned, an 11th century marble low-relief. Bernard Gilduin has represented Christ in a mandorla surrounded by the symbols of the four evangelists.*

▶▶ *Saint-Sernin, 14th century wooden polychrome statues of the apostles. With three other statues of saints, they watch over the entrance to the lower crypt.*

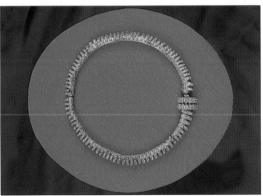

▲▲ *Cinerary urn in the shape of a lidded trough, Musée Saint-Raymond.*

▲ *Gold torque dating from the Volques Tectosages from Fenouillet (Haute-Garonne), Musée Saint-Raymond.*

◀ *Hercules, victorious over Geryon. The Musée Saint-Raymond has several reliefs from the Roman era illustrating the labours of Hercules.*

▶ *Aphrodite of Cnide, Musée Saint-Raymond. One of the best known Roman copies of this famous head!*

MUSÉE SAINT-RAYMOND

B eside the Saint Sernin Basilica, the town's archeological museum is housed in a building resembling a Florentine *palazzo*. False machicolations, crenellated walls and corner towers fit in well with the fine simplicity of its brick structure. Louis Privat, master stone-mason, built this college for poor students in 1523. He also built the superb Bernuy residence. A hospital, founded for pilgrims by Raymond Gayrard, once stood on the site of the college. This canon from Saint-Sernin, who was venerated like a saint, gave his name to the new building. Closed during the Revolution, the college became the Saint-Sernin presbytery. It was made into a museum in 1892 and houses collections of exceptionally high quality covering a period from prehistory to the year one thousand. Exhibits include antique marble sculptures from the Villa Chiragan near Martres-Tolosane, and from Béziers: the labours of Hercules, private portraits and above all, busts of Roman emperors... a set worthy of any museum in Rome! Another treasure of the Musée Saint-Raymond: gold jewellery from the Volques Tectosages, a Celtic people who settled in Toulouse before the Romans. Menhir-statues, objects from the bronze or iron ages, Etruscan coins, Greek vases, funeral monuments... propose a vertiginous trip back in time.

13

◄ *The Jacobins cloister and spire. The South and East galleries have been patiently reconstitued.*

▲▲ *The Jacobins, detail of the cloister. The double marble columns are crowned with capitals with vegetal decorations.*

▲ *The Jacobins, inside the church with its double nave, separated by a row of seven stone columns.*

► *The Jacobins, the keystone of the chapel of Saint-Antonin.*

THE JACOBINS CHURCH AND CONVENT

Who exactly were the Jacobins, founders of this jewel of meriodional Gothic art? No connection with the Jacobins of the Revolution: these were Dominicans, thus called because one of their convents was situated in the Rue Saint-Jacques in Paris. The order of the preaching Friars had been founded in 1215 by Dominique de Guzmán, the future Saint Dominique. He wanted to combat Cathar heresay by the power of the word and the example of a life of poverty... to no avail. And violence prevailed... After his death, the terrible task of the Inquisition was assigned to the Dominicans in 1233... their Order developed and they required a church and a convent. Building work on the church was begun rapidly. The first building was quite modest: a simple rectangle with a wooden roof divided in two by a row of pillars. The congregation had access to the southern part and the Friars used the northern half. The black marble slabs within the present paving mark its location. But the refusal of ostentation was soon forgotten to the benefit of affirming the power of the Church. Firstly, a more imposing chevet was added, then the nave was raised and arched and the belfry heightened. At the same time, the convent was taking shape: chapter house, cloister, refectory, chapel... The power and austerity of the massive brick body, the splendour and

harmony of the double nave with the dizzy height of the extraordinary starred vault…, the Church of the Jacobins, finally completed in 1385, was a masterpiece. In 1368, Pope Urban V decided to have the reliquary of the Dominican Saint Thomas d'Aquin, who had died in Italy in 1274, transferred there: "In the same way as Saint Thomas stands out amongst doctors for the beauty of his style and thought,the church of Toulouse surpasses in beauty all the other churches of the preaching Friars." The Revolution confiscated the Jacobins convent buildings and during the Restoration they were transformed into a barracks: floors raised, nave divided into three parts, windows walled up, walls plastered, two galleries of the cloister destroyed… Prosper Mérimée, who was then Inspector General of Historic Monuments, visited it in 1845 and was indignant at the state of the buildings. The army gave The Jacobins back to the town in 1865. Since then, long restoration campaigns have been carried out. The church has recovered its unity, its splendid vault with bicoloured ribbing, its painted decor and the reliquary of Saint Thomas d'Aquin (which had been removed to Saint-Sernin for safe-keeping).The two missing galleries of the cloister have been entirely rebuilt using elements found in the region. And the chapel of Saint-Antonin is once again decorated with its sumptuous Gothic paintings.

▲▲ *The Jacobins, 14th century fresco from the funeral chapel of Saint-Antonin, representing an episode in the life of the martyr from Pamiers.*

▲ *The vaulted ceiling of the chapter house in the convent of the Jacobins.*

◀ *The Jacobins, reliquary of Saint Thomas d'Aquin, kept under the main altar.*

▶ *The admirable Jacobins "palm tree". At the chevet, the final column supports the arch-springing of the twenty-two ribs of the vault.*

▶▶ *Wall-belfry of Notre-Dame du Taur, characteristic of the Gothic churches in the region.*

▲▲ *Romanesque funeral recess next to the church of Saint-Pierre des Cuisines.*

▲ *The black Virgin with Child (1807) from the church of La Daurade (copy of a Middle Age statue burnt during the Revolution).*

▲ *The church of Saint-Pierre des Chartreux with its lantern dome; viewed through an archway of the convent galleries.*

◀ *Tympanum of the church of Notre-Dame de la Dalbade. Gaston Virebent's highly coloured ceramic contrasts with the severity of the facade.*

▶ *Portal and belfry of the church of the Cordeliers. Very little remains of the convent of the Cordeliers (or Franciscans), a good example of meridional Gothic architecture.*

PAROCHIAL SPIRIT

C atharism, protestantism… Particularly strong religious passions in Toulouse explain the presence of so many institutions asserting the power of the Church. Notre-Dame du Taur, formerly Saint-Sernin du Taur (*taur* from *taureau*, a bull) is a reminder of the the martyrdom of Saint Sernin. According to legend, this Gothic church was built on the site of his first tomb. The *bourgeois* of the town had their increased powers acknowledged by the counts and then by the king at Saint-Pierre des Cuisines, a dependency of the Clunisian Abbey of Moissac. Nearby, the church of Saint-Pierre des Chartreux dates from the 17th and 18th centuries and is richly decorated (high altar, stalls, mural paintings, carved wood, organ…). The massive church of Notre-Dame de la Daurade (from the Latin *deaurata*, golden) takes its name from a 5th century sanctuary decorated with gold mosaics. Its plan was inspired by that of 17th century Roman basilicas. A black Virgin with Child is still worshipped there. Notre-Dame de la Dalbade, built from the wealth gained as a result of the *pastel* trade, was proud to have the highest spire in the town. Destroyed during the Revolution, it was rebuilt in 1881 but collapsed in 1926… Today, its Renaissance portal embellished in 1874 with a highly coloured ceramic, is surprising.

◄ The courtyard of the Assézat residence. This building, in two parts at right angles, which has been wonderfully restored, is a great Renaissance success. Nicolas Bachelier, one of the greatest Toulouse architects at the time, worked on it...

▶ The inside courtyard of the Astorg and Saint-Germain residence, from the second half of the 16th century. Wooden galleries and stairs, one of which seems to be leaning unsupported, give it lots of charm.

▶ The first courtyard of the Bernuy residence dating from 1530. A prodigious flattened compartmented arch supports the carved stone gallery on the right. The Jesuits settled in this residence as early as 1567. Pierre de Fermat (1601-1665), the mathematician famous for his "unprovable" theorem, studied in their college. The present school is named after him.

▶ The Dahus residence. During the 15th century, the "capitoul" Pierre Dahus possessed the large house. One century later, Gauillaume de Tournoër, a parliamentary counsellor, replaced the Gothic tower with a refined Renaissance one.

▶▶ The May residence. In the 16th century, Antoine du May, Queen Margot's doctor, had an elegant residence built. It now houses the Musée du Vieux-Toulouse.

▶▶▶ A mullion window of the residence of the "capitoul" Pierre Comère.

THE LAND OF PLENTY

For a century, Toulouse was rich, very rich, because of the *pastel* trade. From the 15th to the 16th century, magnificent private residences were built in the town, the heart of the *land of plenty*. The *pastel* merchants invested in bricks and, having become *capitouls* (municipal magistrates), they showed off their power by building proud towers. In 1525, Juan de Bernuy, from Burgos, had no difficulty in raising the sum of 1 200 000 écus as bail for François I, held prisoner by Charles V. His sumptuous dwelling, a daring combination of styles, (Gothic, Italian Renaissance, art from the castles of the Loire and Spanish plaster-work), today houses the Pierre de Fermat high-school. Pierre Assézat from Rouergue, another *nouveau riche* who was a *capitoul* twice, had a veritable Renaissance palace built. It remained unfinished however, because of the *pastel* crisis. Its classic facade, with its superposed ancient orders – Doric, Ionic, and Corinthian – is characterised by the alternate use of brick and stone and by other architectural finds: disconnection of the stair tower, octagonal lanternon, cable moulded entrance columns... The Assézat residence now houses various cultural societies – the oldest and most famous being the *Académie des Jeux Floraux*, founded in 1323 – and the Bemberg Foundation's collection of paintings.

21

▲ *The facade of the Capitole stands proudly with its three fore-parts. The left fronton is decorated with statues of Clémence Isaure and Pallas; the right fronton, with representations of Tragedy and Comedy. The middle one is dedicated to Force and Justice.*

◄◄ *The Henri IV courtyard, 17th century.*

◄ *Mullion window of the Henri IV courtyard.*

► *The Capitole, the Great Stairway. Decorated by Laurens.*

IN THE HEART
OF THE CITY

I t took many generations of *capitouls* to achieve the harmonious arrangement of the Place du Capitole (Capitole Square)... the facade which houses the town hall and the Capitole theatre was built between 1750 and 1760 from plans by the Toulouse architect Guillaume Cammas. This noble building, one hundred and seven metres long, with three fore-parts, was simply a glorious screen to hide the group of ill-assorted buildings which then constituted the *Maison commune* (the Town Hall). Eight pink marble columns symbolised the eight *capitouls* who formed the town council. At the time, the Capitole was whitewashed, against the architect's wishes... The subtle show of brick and stone is a reconquest from this century! The construction of the buildings surrounding the square began at the start of the 19th century and the replica of the facade, on the garden side, was completed in 1884... This too was when most of the buildings constituting the former *Maison commune* were taken down. The only ones still standing today: The Henri IV courtyard and the tower of the Capitulary Archives. The galleries of the Henri IV courtyard date from the beginning of the 17th century as does the marble statue of the King himself, one of the rare statues sculpted during his life-time. It was placed in a recess above the sumptuous Renaissance portal which was designed by Nicolas Bachelier. A plaque on the ground in the

courtyard is a reminder of the execution in
1632 of the Duke de Montmorency, Governor
of Languedoc who had opposed Richelieu.
The Archives Tower, today the Donjon du
Capitole (the Capitole Keep), was built in
the 16th century to house the town archives.
It suffered from Viollet-le-Duc's intervention
when he transformed it into a Flemish
belfry... The state rooms in the Town Hall
bear witness to the Golden Age of Toulouse.
The present Salle des Illustres (Hall of
Fame), was arranged in the style of the
Farnèse Gallery in Rome by Paul Pujol at the
end of the 19th century. The decoration
was so heavy that it had to be solidly fixed to
the vaulted roof to prevent the floors from
collapsing... a host of artists from Toulouse
took part its decoration. The Henri Martin
room is decorated with the Impressionist
painter's compositions representing the
seasons and the banks of the Garonne. The
Gervais room, used at one time to celebrate
weddings, is named after the artist who
decorated it with love scenes. The Place du
Capitole has recently been decorated with
an Occitan cross in unpolished bronze,
crowned with signs of the Zodiac by Raymond
Moretti from Nice. This square is the scene
of incessant bustle, but it is not the only
place to attract crowds. With the first rays of
the sun, Place Wilson and its garden and
Place Saint-George and its terraces throng
with meriodional good humour.

◀ *The Capitole, the Salle des Illustres (Hall of Fame). It was redecorated at the end of last century. Sixty-two metres long, it has a series of marble columns and is decorated to excess with ornamental mouldings, sculptures and paintings, typical of the "Belle Époque". Busts of the leading citizens of Toulouse, who have given this majestuous hall its name, still watch over the premises.*

▶ *The Donjon du Capitole (the Capitole Keep), formerly the Archives Tower, with its strange Flemish belfry.*

▲ *The Capitole. The southern end of the Hall of Fame is decorated with a fresco called "Defence of Toulouse against Simon de Montfort", by Jean-Paul Laurens. It depicts the erection of fortifications by the population of Toulouse determined to resist the crusade against the Albigeois.*

◀ *The Capitole, "The Banks of the Garonne" (1903), by Henri Martin, an impressionist painter from Toulouse, is situated in the room which is named after him.*

◀ *The Capitole, the 1324 "Jeux Floraux". The Grand Escalier (Great Staircase) was redecorated in 1912 to harmonise with the style of the state rooms. The artist Jean-Paul Laurens was in charge of the decoration work. His vision of the Middle Ages is a true reflection of the conceptions at the time.*

▶ *Place Wilson was created last century. It is oval and surrounded by neoclassic style buildings. In the centre is a statue of the Occitan poet Goudouli beside a cool fountain.*

◄ *Cloister and church of the Musée des Augustins. Opened to the public in 1795, the Musée des Augustins, then called the "Museum provisoire du Midi de la République" is one of the most ancient and also one of the wealthiest museums in the provinces.*

▶ *12th century Romanesque capital from the destroyed cloister of the Cathedral of Saint Étienne, Musée des Augustins. All round the vase, Gilabertus, one of the rare sculptors of the Middle Ages who signed his work, has depicted the story of Herod and Salome. Here, the death of Saint John the Baptist: the decapitated martyr's soul, represented in the form of a naked child escaping from the body, is welcomed by God.*

▶ *Nostre Dame de Grasse, (Our Lady of Grasse), a 15th century polychrome statue from the convent of the Jacobins, Musée des Augustins. The very young Virgin, whose child seems ready to leave her, looks gently resigned to the destiny of her Son, Saviour of humanity.*

▶ *"Christ and the Two Thieves", Musée des Augustins. It was painted by Rubens at the end of his life in 1635. (He was born in Siegen in 1577 and died at Anvers in 1640). The composition and subject, which accentuate the dramatic aspect of the scene, are typical of the powerful, ostentatious art of this Flemish master who was very successful during his lifetime.*

▶▶ *"Christ with Angels", Van Dijck studio (Anvers 1599 - London 1641), a Flemish painter, disciple of Rubens, Musée des Augustins.*

▶ *A gargoyle from the Church of the Cordeliers (destroyed in 1874) meridional gallery of the cloister of the Musée des Augustins.*

MUSÉE DES AUGUSTINS

O ne of the most beautiful collections of Romanesque capitals in the world, exceptional Gothic sculptures, not to mention a vast panorama of paintings from the 14th to the 19th century... the Musée des Augustins (the Augustins' museum) is not a banal provincial museum. These marvels are presented in a superb setting: the former convent of the hermit Brethern of Saint-Augustin (14th and 15th centuries). The rooms dedicated to the Middle Ages open onto a peaceful cloister guarded by gargoyles, the last ghosts of the church of the Cordeliers... The Romanesque sculpture room exhibits extraordinary capitals saved from destroyed cloisters in Toulouse (Herod's Feast, Marie the Egyptian, the Three Wise Men...). In the chapel of Notre-Dame de Pitié (Our Lady of Pity), the statues of the former chapel of Rieux show the virtuosity of the 14th century sculptors. The highlight of the chapter house, *Nostre Dame de Grasse* (Our Lady of Grasse), a delicate Virgin and child dating from the 15th century is a a masterpiece of gentleness. *Christ and the Two Thieves* by Rubens and *Christ with the Angels* from Van Dijck's studio have places of honour in the church. On the first floor are the works of artists as varied as Canaletto, Pérugin, Guardi, Madame Vigée-Lebrun, Subleyras, Delacroix, Courbet, Corot, Ingres, Manet, Vuillard, Toulouse-Lautrec... and some Toulouse artists.

▲ *Cathedral of Saint Étienne, detail of the wrought iron railings enclosing the choir. They were done in 1767 by the locksmith Bernard Ortet.*

▶ *Place Saint-Étienne, the "Griffoul" fountain and the unusual Cathedral of Saint Étienne with its 16th century bell tower adjacent to a Gothic facade. The portal, strangely offset in relation to the rose-window, gives access to a huge nave characteristic of the beginning of meridional Gothic style. It is called the "Raymond VI" nave because its construction was begun when he was Count of Toulouse; it was not completed until after his death.*

AIVD. E. MANVS. SIC VINCI ET VINCERE. PVLCHRVM EST. & OVA VBI VICTORI.

◀ *Cathedral of Saint Étienne, detail of the tapestries decorating the nave representing Saint Étienne in meditation. This set was ordered during the 17th century to decorate the nave, the choir and the cloister.*

▶ *Romanesque-Gothic house, rue Croix-Baragnon. Built in the 13th century, this residence was unfortunately altered in the 17th century; however, it has retained its elegant twinned windows surmounted by a small circular window and its carved supporting stones.*

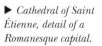

▲ *Cathedral of Saint Étienne, interior of the choir in septentrional Gothic style with, in the foreground, the enormous column which Archbishop Jean d'Orléans had erected in the 16th century to link the nave and the choir.*

▶ *Cathedral of Saint Étienne, detail of a Romanesque capital.*

THE CATHEDRAL OF SAINT ÉTIENNE

This cathedral is the result of nearly one thousand years of effort; it has a strange charm combining eras and styles in a huge jig-saw puzzle of stone and brick... As early as the 11th century, Bishop Isarn replaced a paleochristian building by a Romanesque church and had convent buildings built – including a very beautiful cloister, demolished in the 19th century. At the beginning of the 13th century, Bishop Foulque de Marseille began another construction: a very wide nave with a diagonally ribbed vault . In 1272, Bishop Bertrand de l'Isle-Jourdain dreamt of an enormous stone nave like those in the North of France. When he died in 1286, the choir of the new cathedral stood beside the former nave... but the new nave was never built... In the 16th century, Archbishop Jean d'Orléans resigned himself to linking the two dissimilar buildings by means of an immense column and had the belfry built. At the beginning of the 17th century, following a fire, the choir was given a vaulted roof and the furniture was renewed. Finally, in the 20th century, the North door was arranged. Place Saint-Étienne (Saint Étienne's Square), was thus called as early as 1216 when Simon de Montfort's crusaders fought against the people of Toulouse in the Rue Croix-Baragnon. This elegant street has retained some beautiful ancient residences, including a mediaeval house in Romanesque-Gothic style, one of the oldest in the town.

◀ *The old slaughter house on the banks of the river Garonne now houses the Modern Art Museum and the Toulouse Centre for Contemporary Art. The museum presents a vast panorama of modern art from Soulages to the Gutaï group and includes Tàpies, Dubuffet, Matta, Takis, Hartung…*

▶ *"The red and yellow apples" (detail), Pierre Bonnard, Bemberg Foundation. One entire room is dedicated to the works of Bonnard (1867-1947) and of Vuillard (1868-1940).*

▶ *"The Marie-Christine Baths at Sainte-Adresse" (1903), Raoul Dufy, Bemberg Foundation. In this work the first fruits of his fauvist technique are noticeable.*

▶▶ *A funeral barque in polychrome wood, Middle Empire (2065-1785 B.C.) Musée Georges-Labit. The Egyptian tombs contained model boats with their crews, which were to enable the deceased to cross to the next world.*

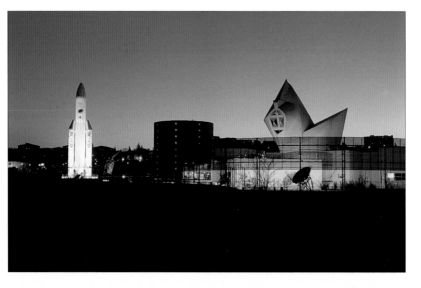

◀ *The Cité de l'Espace, at night. Ariane 5 and the Mir station are to be found amongst other exhibits in the grounds.*

▶ *The macroscope. It presents various views of the Earth, from the first geographical maps to recent satellite pictures. The different elements of space adventure can be found at the Cité: a rocket launch, satellite communication, meteorology… and an approach to such phenomena as the Coriolis effect and weightlessness.*

CITY OF SPACE
AND OF THE ARTS

P aul Dupuy (1867-1944), Georges Labit (1862-1899), Georges Bemberg…, the names of these patrons of the arts are very much alive in Toulouse. Their precious collections are exhibited in very pleasant surroundings. The Musée Paul-Dupuy is dedicated to the decorative arts. Many objects and works of art dating from the Middle Ages to the present day are exhibited, including an 11th century ivory horn, a 13th century astrolabe, a 17th century carved wood medicine-chest and an exceptional set of watches and clocks dating from the 16th to the 19th century. Asian and Middle Eastern art is the main theme of the Musée Georges-Labit. The Moorish villa of this great traveller houses some marvels. The Assézat residence houses the possessions of the Bemberg Foundation. 16th and 17th century paintings and from the modern French school ancient objects, bronzes and books. The Modern Art Museum also boasts an astonishing scenic curtain - a 14 metre by 20 metre gouache - painted by Picasso for Raymond Roland's play « The 14th of July ». At the Museum of Ancient Toulouse, a thousand souvenirs provide a key to Golden Age of the *Pink City*. As European space capital, Toulouse was the obvious choice for the location of a site dedicated to space sciences and technology. In 1997, the Space City was opened. Here, the approach to the fascinating universe which surrounds us, is both didactic and fun.

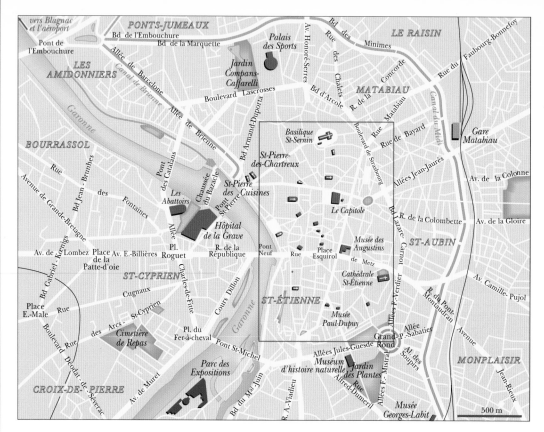

vers Blagnac
et l'aéroport

PONTS-JUMEAUX
Bd de l'Embouchure
Bd de la Marquette

Pont de
l'Embouchure

LES
AMIDONNIERS

Allée de Barcelone

Canal de Brienne

Allée de Brienne

Boulevard Lascrosses

Jardin
Compans-
Caffarelli

Palais
des Sports

LE RAISIN

Av. Honoré-Serres

Rue des

Minimes

Concorde

Bd des

Chalets

Bd d'Arcole

R. de la

MATABIAU

Rue Matabiau

Canal du Midi

Rue du Faubourg-Bonnefoy

Gare
Matabiau

Garonne

BOURRASSOL

Rue

Bd Jean- Brunhes

Avenue de Grande-Bretagne

des

Fontaines

Pont
des Catalans

Chaussée
du Bazacle

Les
Abattoirs

Pont
St-Pierre

St-Pierre
des Cuisines

Bd Armand-Duporta

Basilique
St-Sernin

St-Pierre-
des-Chartreux

Boulevard de Strasbourg

Rue de Bayard

Allées Jean-Jaurès

Av. de la Colonne

Allée

Hôpital
de la Grave

Le Capitole

Bd Lazare- Carnot

R. de la Colombette

Av. de la Gloire

Av. de -Lombez
Place Av. E.-Billières
de la
Patte-d'oie

Pl.
Roguet

R. de la
République

Pont
Neuf

Place
Esquirol

Musée des
Augustins

ST-AUBIN

Bd Gabriel - Koenig

ST-CYPRIEN

Charles-de-Fitte

Rue

de Metz

Cathédrale
St-Étienne

Allées F.-Verdier

R. du Pont-
Montaudran

Av. Camille- Pujol

Place
E.-Male

Rue

Cugnaux

St-Cyprien

Cours Dillon

ST-ÉTIENNE

Musée
Paul-Dupuy

Allées-P.-Sabatier

Allée

Avenue

Boulevard Déodat- de -Séverac

Rue

des Arcs

Cimetière
de Repas

Pl. du
Fer-à-cheval

Pont St-Michel

Garonne

Allées Jules-Guesde

Grand- Rond

Al. des
Soupirs

MONPLAISIR

CROIX-DE-PIERRE

Av. de Muret

Parc des
Expositions

Bd du Mal-Juin

Muséum
d'histoire naturelle

Jardin
des Plantes

Rue Alfred-Duméril

Allées F.- Mistral

R. A.-Nadieu

Musée
Georges-Labit

Jean-Rieux

500 m

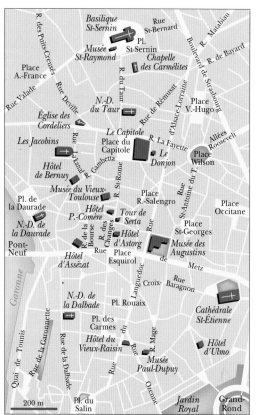

R. des Petits-Creusés

Basilique
St-Sernin

Rue
St-Bernard

Rue Matabiau

Place
A.-France

Musée
St-Raymond

Pl.
St-Sernin

Chapelle
des Carmélites

R. du Taur

Boulevard de Strasbourg

R. de Bayard

Rue Valade

Rue Deville

N.-D.
du Taur

Rue de Rémusat

Place
V.-Hugo

Rue d'Alsace-Lorraine

Église des
Cordeliers

Les Jacobins

Rue

le canal

R. Gambetta

Le Capitole
Place du
Capitole

R. La Fayette

Le
Donjon

Place
Wilson

Allées Roosevelt

Hôtel
de Bernuy

Musée du Vieux-
Toulouse

R. St-Rome

Place
R.-Salengro

Rue St-Antoine du T.

Place
Occitane

Pl. de
la Daurade

Hôtel
P.-Comère

Tour de
Serta

Place
St-Georges

N.-D. de
la Daurade

R. de
la Bourse

R. des
Changes

Hôtel
d'Astorg

Rue

Place
de Metz

Musée des
Augustins

Pont-
Neuf

Hôtel
d'Assézat

Rue

Place
Esquirol

Languedoc

Croix-
Baragnon

Garonne

N.-D. de
la Dalbade

Pl. Rouaix

R. Mage

Cathédrale
St-Étienne

Quai de Tounis

Rue de la Garonnette

Pl. des
Carmes

du

Hôtel
d'Ulmo

Hôtel du
Vieux-Raisin

Rue

Rue

Rue de la Dalbade

Rue

Ozenne

Musée
Paul-Dupuy

200 m

Pl. du
Salin

Jardin
Royal

Grand-
Rond

CONTENTS